NORTH LONDON RAILWAY
OPEN AIR ROUTE
NON-STOP
TRAINS
... FROM ...
HAMPSTEAD

BROAD ST

CITY and		Mins.
GOSPEL OAK	- -	14
HAMPSTEAD	- -	16
FINCHLEY ROAD	-	19

FRANK REE General Manager

HAMPSTEAD

PAST & PRESENT

Heath Street with the fire station in the centre, *c.* 1905.

BRITAIN

IN OLD PHOTOGRAPHS

HAMPSTEAD

PAST & PRESENT

CLIVE & DAVID SMITH

Sutton Publishing Limited
Phoenix Mill · Thrupp · Stroud
Gloucestershire · GL5 2BU

First published 2002

Copyright © Clive and David Smith, 2002

British Library Cataloguing in Publication Data
A catalogue record for this book is available from the
British Library.

ISBN 0-7509-2915-4

Typeset in 10.5/13.5 Photina.
Typesetting and origination by
Sutton Publishing Limited.
Printed and bound in England by
J.H. Haynes & Co. Ltd, Sparkford.

Front Endpaper: The Viaduct, Hampstead Heath, *c.* 1920. Young boys are throwing stones into the water.
Half-title page photograph: J. Buckingham & Sons dairy cart, from Fairfax Road, South Hampstead, *c.* 1905.
Title page photograph: St John Ambulance on Hampstead Heath, *c.* 1903.
Back Endpaper: The Viaduct, Hampstead, 2002.

Bank Holiday revellers outside the Bull and Bush, *c.* 1903.

CONTENTS

Vale of Health Hotel, *c.* 1903.

St John's parish church, Church Row, *c*. 1900.

INTRODUCTION

Hampstead, 'an amiable, elevated lubberland, affording to London the example of a kind of suburban Nirvana'

Wilkie Collins, 1824–89

Hampstead's name is derived from the old English *heam*, meaning a home, and *stede*, a place. The Manor of Hampstead was granted to the Abbey of Westminster in AD 986 and the Domesday Book confirms that the manor was still held by Westminster in 1086. It was eventually surrendered to Henry VIII during the Dissolution of the Monasteries in 1539, shortly after which, in 1540, it became part of the endowment of the new Westminster bishopric. This was short lived, however: when the bishopric was reduced to a deanery Hampstead reverted to the Crown. From 1550 onwards there was a succession of owners, culminating with the Maryon-Wilson family. Although still a small village, Hampstead became famous in the early eighteenth century as a popular resort.

The cause of the transformation of a quiet London suburb into a fashionable resort was the 'mineral springs', like those that attracted vast numbers of people to Bath, Cheltenham and Tunbridge Wells in order to take the waters. The period of the greatest popularity of these Hampstead wells was in the early part of the eighteenth century, when various physicians made extravagant claims for the water as a cure-all. In 1700 an advertisement appeared in *The Postman*: 'The Chalybeate water at Hampstead, being of the same nature and equal virtues with Tunbridge Wells, sold by Mr Richard Philps, apothecary at the Eagle and Child in Fleet Street every morning at 3*d* per flask and conveyed to persons at their own houses for 1*d* more. The flask to be returned daily.'

Hampstead was famous enough in the early eighteenth century to be the location of a comedy, performed at the Drury Lane Theatre, in which it is referred to as a 'Sweet rural spot where business is lain fast asleep, a variety of diversions feast on fickle fancies, and every man wears a face of pleasure. The cards fly, the dice rattle . . .' One of the characters (Arabella) is represented as saying: 'Well this Hampstead's a charming place to come to dance all night at the Wells.'

It became a favourite place for artists and writers. In 1749 Dr Samuel Johnson wrote part of *The Vanity of Human Wishes* here. John Keats lived part of his short life in Well Walk and John Street – now Keats Grove. Other notable Hampstead residents

Phil May's cartoon "'Appy 'Ampstead', *c.* 1898.

included George Romney, John Constable, John Linnell, Mark Akenside, J.H. Leigh Hunt, Joanna Baillie, John Galsworthy, H.G. Wells, Stanley Spencer, Kate Greenaway and Phil May.

According to James Park in his *History of Hampstead*, written in 1814 and reprinted in 1818: 'Hampstead was, in the time of Henry VIII, inhabited largely by washerwomen, and here the clothes of the nobility and gentry were brought from London to be washed.' Park observed: 'from an obscure hamlet, principally occupied by laundresses, Hampstead arose into a crowded and fashionable resort, teeming with amusements, folly and dissipation. However, from the bustling population and indiscriminate association of a watering-place, it has at length subsided into a much better thing. The permanent residence of a select amicable, respectable and opulent neighbourhood.'

In the nineteenth century, after the development of Regent's Park and the arrival of the railways, urbanisation began to take place. The most significant years of Hampstead's history are probably from 1829 until 1871. During this period residents fought a battle to preserve the Heath as an open space. Finally the then Lord of the Manor, Sir John Maryon-Wilson, and his family agreed to sell this land to the Metropolitan Board of Works for £47,000. Some 240 acres were dedicated for the use of the public in 1872. Including later acquisitions, Parliament Hill Fields, Golders Hill, the Heath Extension and Ken Wood, the Heath totals over 800 acres of land for the use of the public.

Date		Acreage	Initial Cost
1872	Hampstead Heath	240½	£47,000
1884–5	Parliament Hill Fields	267½	£302,000
1898	Golders Hill	36	£38,500
1904	Heath Extension	80	£36,000
1922–4	Ken Wood Estate	121	£152,124
1925–7	Ken Wood Mansion and Grounds	89	(gift of the 1st Earl of Iveagh)
	Totals	**834**	**£575,624**

In 1840 a uniform national Penny Post was introduced, the first in the world. Sir Rowland Hill was also responsible for the world's first adhesive postage stamp, the famous 'Penny Black'. He lived in Pond Street, Hampstead, for many years.

A letter posted from Hampstead on 19 September 1840.

Jack Straw's Castle, *c.* 1900.

Many books have been written about this well-loved area of London, and it is interesting to note what was being remarked on in 1876:

Hampstead, Middlesex, famous for its Heath, pure air and its fine scenery, lies north by west of London on the outer edge of the Metropolitan Boundary. The 4 mile circle cuts the southern slope of the hill on which the village is built, and the 4½ mile stone is at the commencement of the Heath, north of the town.

The Heath being a great pleasure resort, Hampstead abounds in Inns; those about the Heath are The Castle (better known as Jack Straw's Castle) on the summit an excellent house; The Vale of Health Hotel, in the hollow to the east; The Spaniards by the lane leading to Highgate and the Bull and Bush, North End.

Hampstead stands on one of the highest hills around London. The town occupies its southern slopes, the Heath its summit, which is 443 feet above sea level. The town straggles up the slopes of the hill towards the Heath at the top in an odd, sidelong, torturous, irregular and unconnecting fashion. There is the fairly broad winding High Street and other good streets and lanes, lined with large old brick built houses within high walled enclosures, over which lean ancient trees.

James Thorne's *Environs of London*

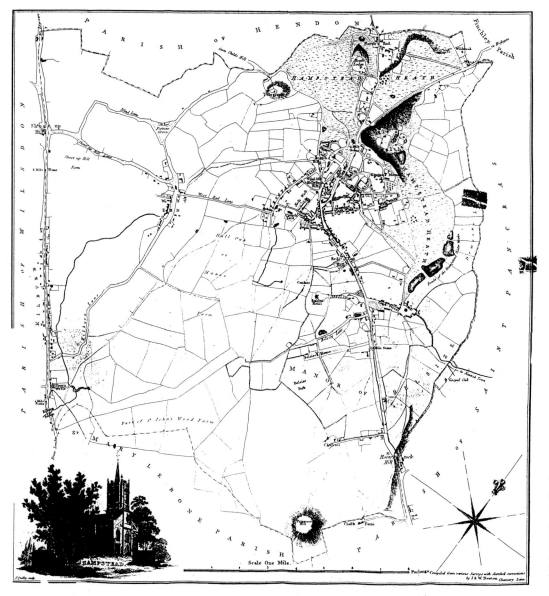

This map is taken from *The Topography and Natural History of Hampstead* by John James Park, 1818.

Nearly all the old photographs in this book date from 1900 to 1910. This is a near-contemporary piece written in 1898 by Mr Vizard in his book *A Guide to Hampstead*:

Hampstead Has Retained So Much of its Old Charm

The vast and modern growth of London in recent years, together with modern 'improvements', has made sad havoc of many quaint and interesting spots, both in the centre and suburbs of London.

    Radiating out in all directions, the mighty stream has crept, and is creeping, year by year, like a baleful lava-flow, obliterating fair fields, with their flowers, hedgerows, and stiles – loved haunts of our childhood; sweeping away quaint and picturesque old houses, with their red tiles and gabled roofs, under the inexorable demands of modern 'improvements', or modern greed; there being too often substituted in their place prosaic villas, or huge and unsightly blocks of 'flats'.

Hampstead, like every other part of London, has suffered in this respect – suffered greatly; still, it may well be doubted whether any other part of London has suffered less. Certainly no place within the same easy distance of the City has retained so much of its old charm, so many of its ancient objects of interest, of its quaint nooks and byways, as Hampstead. Our priceless Heath has arrested, in one direction at least, the fell stream of building, and we have for our boundary and outlook, in this quarter, as large a tract of pure and beautiful as can be found anywhere round London. The delightful pasture-fields between Hampstead and Highgate are untouched, and happily will remain so. Most of the upper part of the old town also remains as it was – most, but not all – and nowhere round London will you find remaining such fine old houses with large gardens, such quaint and old-fashioned nooks and corners, and unexpected turnings, such sudden dips and rapid ascents, as are to be found in what is still left of old Hampstead.

Parliament approved a scheme for the construction of an Underground Electric Railway from Charing Cross (Strand) to Hampstead as early as 1893. However, ten years were to pass before work began in 1903.

The financial backing for this project came from an American financier, Charles Tyson Yerkes (pronounced Yerkees), who came to London in 1900 and took over the company constructing the Hampstead tube (now the Northern line). It was Yerkes who foresaw development north of Hampstead and chose Golders Green as a terminus instead of Hampstead, as originally intended.

The extension was given parliamentary approval in 1902 and tunnelling commenced in 1903. Yerkes died in 1905, two years before completion. The new tube line opened on Saturday 22 June 1907, when David Lloyd George, MP and President of the Board of Trade, started the first train.

Strange as it may seem, and unknown to many people who travel daily on the Northern line, there is a station that was partly built but never completed. It lies between Hampstead and Golders Green and was intended to be called North End, later changed to

The Bull and Bush
Hotel, *c.* 1895.

The Spaniards Inn,
c. 1895.

the Bull and Bush – as its surface station would have been behind this old inn. The platforms were constructed and are there to this day. The Bull and Bush station has been used for a variety of purposes, including the safe storage of archives during the Second World War.

In the fourteenth century the Belsize estate was a sub-manor of Hampstead. The first lords of the manor were a family called Waad, who leased the property from Westminster.

In 1663 the old Belsize House was rebuilt at some expense by a Colonel Daniel O'Neill, who married Lady Chesterfield. The estate remained in the ownership of the Chesterfield family for over a century. During the eighteenth century the house and park were leased out to various tenants, and it was during this period that it achieved a certain notoriety as an extravagant pleasure resort. Finally in 1807 the Chesterfield family sold Belsize House, with its park and some 230 acres, to four local men. It was then divided up for development. However, the old house was not demolished until 1841.

In 1900 Hampstead Heath was still the beginning of the countryside. The green fields of Golders Green were largely unblemished, apart from a little cluster of cottages near the White Swan, in Golders Green Road, and the odd farm building. However, this was soon to change with the construction of the Hampstead tube and the siting of the terminus at Golders Green in 1907. With the development of Golders Green, Hampstead was encircled and the Heath assumed an even greater importance.

On 1 April 1965 the Metropolitan Borough of Hampstead was amalgamated with the Boroughs of St Pancras and Holborn to form what is now the London Borough of Camden.

A complete history of Hampstead, whether in photographs or words, could not be fitted into one volume. To find out more one must refer to the many excellent books available at the public library or the bookshop.

1
North End

Wyldes Farm, North End. *c.* 1900. North End is so called because of its situation at the extremity of the Heath. Collins or Tooley's Farm, North End, is now known by its old name of Wyldes. John Linnell, painter and benefactor of William Blake, lived here in 1823. The Heath extension (Wyldes farmland) was purchased by grants from authorities and subscriptions from the public. Around 80 acres were added to the Heath in 1904.

North End Village, looking towards Golders Green, *c.* 1905. Sandy Road is on the left. *Opposite*: the same view today.

The Bull and Bush was made famous by the music hall song, 'Down at the Old Bull and Bush', popularised by the music hall comedienne Florrie Forde. It was once said that when Florrie Forde sang a chorus number it was 'made'. She sang 'Down at the Old Bull and Bush' – and the rest of us have been singing it with gusto ever since. The photographs date from *c.* 1912 and 2002.

Opening of the

HAMPSTEAD TUBE

SATURDAY, JUNE 22, 1907.

ALIGHT AT

Golders Green

Five minutes' walk to

"Y^e Old^e Bull & Bush"

FOR

GOOD

Dinners and Teas

A BAND will play from 5 till 8.

OPEN-AIR CONCERT

In the Beautiful Gardens,
Illuminated with Fairy Lamps, at **8.15**

Admission 6d.   Numbered & Reserved Seat 1/-

Telephone: 1685 (P.O.) Hampstead.

The Hare and Hounds, *c.* 1908. German bombs destroyed this building during air attacks in 1940. A temporary building was used for many years until it was rebuilt in 1966. Today it is going through another change.

Jack Straw's Castle, 1907. Near the summit of the heath, 440ft above sea level, the inn dates back to at least 1713. Legend has it that Jack Straw, one of Wat Tyler's men in the peasants' revolt in 1381, met his followers here. Charles Dickens wrote of it to his friend John Forster: 'I know of a good house where we can have a red-hot chop for dinner and a glass of good wine.'

   The building was badly damaged by German landmines during air attacks in 1940–1. It was completely rebuilt in 1962. Today the windows are boarded up prior to it being converted into luxury apartments.

The Whitestone Pond, *c.* 1930. Originally a horse pond, it would have been a welcome sight for the horses that had climbed to the highest point of the Heath. The picture above shows the pond being used mainly as a boating lake: it was a centre of activity, and for many years there were donkey rides. *Below*: the scene today. A father and his sons with two remote controlled speedboats.

2

The Village

Heath Street, looking towards High Street, *c.* 1906. The spire of the Baptist church can be seen in the centre of the picture. Heath Street, one of the oldest streets in Hampstead, formed part of the old village. When this photo was taken Hampstead was very much a town, with its own town hall. However, this part of Hampstead is still referred to as the Village.

Holly Hill, *c.* 1910. The artist George Romney lived here from 1734 until 1802. It was purchased in 1806–7 by the trustees of the newly formed Assembly Rooms Committee and altered to accommodate dinners and assemblies. Today the building is a private residence.

The Holly Bush Tavern, *c*. 1900. Converted from the stables and outbuildings of Romney's house in the early part of the nineteenth century, it was used as an entrance and for refreshments for the visitors to the Assembly Rooms.

Mount Vernon Hospital, *c.* 1915. The hospital took its name from General Charles Vernon who owned property in the area in 1785. The building, which dates from the early nineteenth century, was originally a hospital for patients suffering from consumption. It has recently been converted into luxury apartments.

Church Row, looking towards the parish church of St John, 1906. This delightful row of Georgian houses dates from about 1720, and the church of St John was rebuilt between 1745 and 1747, to designs by John Sanderson. Many notable people are buried in its churchyard, including John Constable.

This page and opposite: The Everyman Theatre opened on 15 September 1920, having been converted from the Hampstead Drill Hall of the 3rd Middlesex Rifle Volunteer Corps. It was later converted once more, this time into a cinema under the guidance of local man Martin Fairfax Jones, and re-opened on 26 December 1933 with a showing of René Clair's *The Million*. It is still a cinema today, and plans are afoot to upgrade the venue further.

Heath Street, *c.* 1905. The fire station, now occupied by the Nationwide Building Society, was built in 1873 – the fourth opened by the Metropolitan Fire Brigade. The observation post at the top of the tower had to be removed for safety reasons.

The Hampstead tube. A company formed in 1893 to build a tube railway from Charing Cross to Heath Street failed to raise sufficient money. When US financier Charles Tyson Yerkes bought the rights in 1900 for £100,000 he also secured substantial backing from other wealthy Americans. His experience of American railways and the possibilities of opening up new areas to development led him to change the terminus from Heath Street to the open spaces of Golders Green. The tunnels between Hampstead and Golders Green were started from both ends, and when they met at a point about 100 yards north of Heath Street the error was only three-quarters of an inch! At Heath Street the railway lines are almost 200ft below ground. The new tube line was opened in June 1907, when David Lloyd George, then President of the Board of Trade, started the first train. Travel was free that day and 140,000 people took advantage of this.

High Street, from the junction with Heath Street, *c.* 1930. The Hampstead tube station is still very much the same today.

High Street, looking towards Rosslyn Hill, *c.* 1909. An advertisement on the wooden-fronted building is for a building site to let or for lease. The photographer has captured a wonderfully animated Edwardian street scene. This is contrasted with a typically busy midweek scene in 2002.

High Street, looking towards Holly Hill, 1903. The Bird in Hand public house on the right, which was the terminus for the horse-buses, is now Café Rouge, with two floors of continental-style refreshments.

High Street, looking towards Heath Street and Holly Hill, 1920s. The old fire station, pictured above, was occupied at this time by Hampton's estate agents. In 2002 the fire station is occupied by a building society. The paved entrance to Flask Walk is on the right.

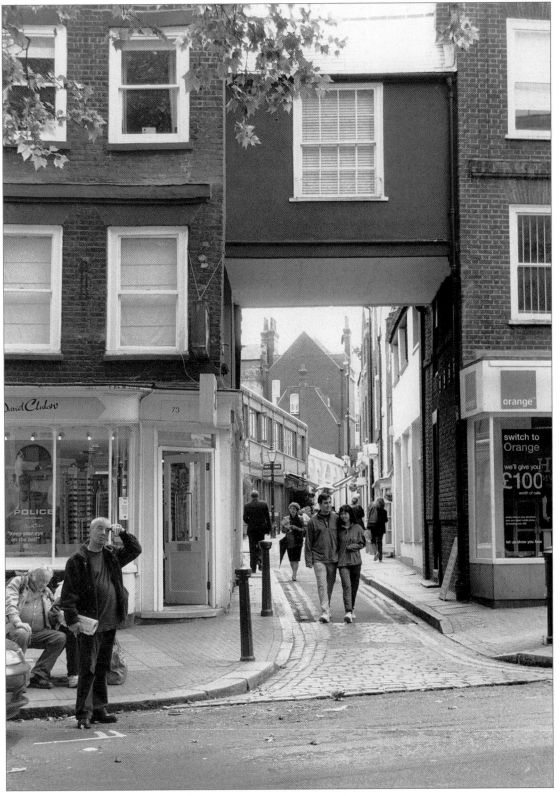

This page and opposite: Entrance to Perrins Court from the High Street, *c.* 1908. Two well-established shops flank the entrance to the walkway. Forster's, on the left, was founded in 1790 and Skoyles, on the right, dates from 1829. Both have now changed hands.

Above left: Flask Walk as it was in 1902, showing the two-storey building over the entrance into the High Street. This building was demolished in 1911.
Above: the view from High Street, February 1911.
Left: the same spot today.

Flask Walk, at the Well Walk end, 1905. The building on the right was the Flask Walk Baths and Laundry, built by the Wells and Campden Trust in 1888 to encourage cleanliness. This building was converted to residential use in the 1970s.

The White Bear public house, New End, *c.* 1904. This inn is one of the oldest in Hampstead, dating from 1704. The White Bear still retains its name and character today.

The Flask public house, *c.* 1908 and today. The Flask takes its name from when waters from the chalybeate springs were bottled here, in 1700.

Well Walk, *c.* 1907. Well Walk takes its name from the springs which brought fame and fashion to the area. This picture shows the Victorian fountain, which commemorates the chalybeate well. Chalybeate water was impregnated with iron.

Wells Tavern, c. 1908. It is situated on the corner of Well Road and Christchurch Hill. Built in about 1830, it is a reminder of the wells that made Hampstead a spa to rival Tunbridge Wells.

Christ Church in Hampstead Square, with its graceful and dominating spire, was built in 1851. Its architect, Samuel Whitfield Dawkes, also designed St Andrews, Well Street and St Marylebone, which was later moved piece by piece to Kingsbury. His other work included some railway stations and Colney Hatch Hospital.

Burgh House, New End Square, was built in 1703. A physician named William Gibbons lived here in 1720 and his initials still grace its wrought-iron gates. Allatson Burgh, of St Lawrence Jewry (1769–1856), came to live in this house in 1822. He is reputed to have added a music room. Burgh was a member of the committee whose protest in 1829 led to the withdrawal in the House of Commons of the lord of the manor's private bill to permit building on Hampstead Heath. In 1858 the house was taken over by the Royal East Middlesex Militia. A more recent tenant was Elsie Bambridge, Rudyard Kipling's daughter. Kipling's last outing before his death in 1936 was to Burgh House. After surviving the bombs of the Second World War the house was bought by Hampstead Borough Council in 1947. In 1977 the building was threatened by dry rot. Residents formed the Burgh House Trust and raised £50,000. The house was restored by Camden Council, leased to the Trust and opened to the public in 1979 as a meeting place, exhibition centre and museum.

High Street, looking towards the future site of the tube station, 1902. On the left were the offices of the *Hampstead and Highgate Express*, now the post office. *Below*: the continual stream of traffic filing up the High Street, 2002.

High Street, looking towards Rosslyn Hill, 1902. The Wesleyan chapel on the corner of Prince Arthur Road was demolished in 1935. Today the Victorian letterbox, which is preserved as an ancient monument, is sealed shut. However, Hampstead post office is only a few yards away on the other side of the street.

The High Street, looking towards Rosslyn Hill, 1905. The King of Bohemia public house is on the left. A horse-bus is struggling up the hill. Note the third horse that was added to the team to help on the long pull up from Chalk Farm. The church tower in the centre of the picture belonged to the Trinity Presbyterian church. Built in 1862, it was demolished in 1962.

Rosslyn Hill, *c.* 1903. On the left behind the shops lies the Rosslyn Hill chapel, founded in 1692 – a Unitarian Church.

Haverstock Hill, *c.* 1903. Passengers are boarding a horse-bus outside St Stephen's Church, which dates from 1870. It is in French Gothic style, built of purple Luton bricks with granite and stone dressings. The architect was Samuel Sanders Teulon. In recent years the church has been closed because of structural problems. *Below*: in 2002 a line of taxis take a break near their shelter.

Haverstock Hill and St Stephen's Church. This road stretches from Rosslyn Hill to Chalk Farm Road. The origins of the name are obscure. The Express Dairy building is now a fast food outlet and the Hampstead Green post office is a restaurant.

Hampstead Green, 1905, showing the entrance to Hampstead General Hospital which was replaced by the Royal Free Hospital in 1974. It is now a cobbled walkway to the hospital.

The George public house, on the corner of Haverstock Hill and Rowland Hill Street. Sir Rowland Hill, the originator of the Penny Post in 1840, lived on Hampstead Green. Today the pub is called the Rat and Parrot.

Rosslyn Hill from Downshire Hill, *c.* 1905. Rosslyn Hill was originally known as Red Lion Hill after a pub of that name.

Downshire Hill, *c.* 1905. The picture shows the postal sorting office and postmen. At this time there were over 100 postmen based in Hampstead. Today the building is occupied by the Keats Group Practice.

East Heath Road, looking towards South End Green, with Downshire Hill on the right, *c.* 1914. On the left there is now a car park, hidden behind the trees.

The Freemasons Arms, Downshire Hill, *c.* 1905. Rebuilt in the 1930s, at that time it had the only pell mell court in the country. Pell mell is a game similar to croquet, and involves passing a large heavy ball through hoops without a mallet. The Freemasons also has a skittle alley in the cellar: the game is played by throwing a cheese at the pins. The Hampstead Lawn Billiard Club run the alley on Tuesday and Saturday evenings.

St John's Church,
Downshire Hill, *c.* 1907.
The architect and builder
was William Woods and
the church was
consecrated in 1823.
Downshire Hill, once
called The Brickfield, is a
well-known example of
villa development from
the nineteenth century.

Lawn Bank, now known as Keats House. The house dates from 1815–16. It was here in the spring of 1819 that John Keats wrote 'Ode to a Nightingale'. In 1920 the house was put up for sale and a campaign was launched to purchase it as a memorial to Keats. The £10,000 was raised, with more than £2,500 coming from the United States, and the house opened to the public in 1925. Inset is a newspaper cutting from 5 April 1920.

The Load of Hay public house, Haverstock Hill, *c.* 1910. The pub was rebuilt in 1863 and was used by horse-drawn coaches to take a rest from the steep hill. It is currently being refurbished internally.

Haverstock Hill near the junction with Prince of Wales Road, 1903. The church on the corner was the Oxenden Presbyterian church, built in 1877. It was acquired in 1970 by the Seventh Day Adventist Church and was re-opened in January 1972.

East Heath Road with Squires Mount on the right, *c.* 1920. The same scene was photographed in 2002 from the Vale of Health.

Fishing in the Vale of Health pond, Edwardian-style. The Vale of Health Hotel was built in the nineteenth century and demolished in 1967. It was strongly criticised by William Howitt in his book *The Northern Heights of London*, published in 1869: 'Recent times have seen Sunday dissipation reasserting itself, by the erection of a monster public house with a lofty tower and flag, to attract the attention of Sunday strollers on the Heath. Of all places, this raised its Tower of Babel bulk in that formerly quiet and favourite spot, the Vale of Health.' The hotel was replaced by a block of flats, which was named after the artist Stanley Spencer: he had his studio on the top floor of the hotel for many years. When today's photograph was taken fishing was suspended as wildfowl were nesting on the pond.

Fishing at Hampstead Ponds, *c.* 1938 and, still as popular as ever, in 2002.

Easter Sunday on Hampstead Heath, *c.* 1905. This is the calm before the storm. The photograph is contrasted with a scene from June 2002, the bank holiday for Queen Elizabeth II's Golden Jubilee. All the rides are covered, waiting for opening time.

The cinematograph, *c.* 1910. This was a travelling cinema at the Hampstead bank holiday fair. The fairground operators were quick to seize on the new invention. On the bank holiday for Queen Elizabeth's Golden Jubilee in 2002 Hampstead Fair was still as popular as ever.

3

South End Green

A horse-drawn tram, which travelled from Euston to Hampstead. South End Green was still a small hamlet until the mid-nineteenth century, when the arrival of the railway forced the demolition of some of the houses. Following this, permission for the London Street Tramway to bring its horse-trams to South End Green was granted, and so it became one of the main entrances into Hampstead, and especially the Heath.

Hampstead Heath station in its heyday.
The station, which opened on 2 January
1860, was the scene of a disaster in 1892.
The Easter bank holiday brought the usual
crowds to the Heath for the fun fair, but
heavy rain forced many to dash for shelter
in the station. Eight people were crushed to
death and many were injured on a
staircase leading to the platform. The old
station has been demolished and replaced
with a new building, which is set back off
the road.

South End Road, *c.* 1923. The Railway Tavern on the right is now called the Garden Gate, and the railway coal-yard has been converted into housing.

South End Green, *c.* 1905. Pond Street is on the left and the fountain is on The Green. The fountain was a gift to the people in 1880 by Miss Anne Crump of Hereford House, which made way for the Picture House in 1918. Two horse-drawn trams are seen in the picture above.

Station Parade, South End Road, *c.* 1908. A line of horse-drawn hackney carriages wait for customers. Rumbold's bakery is on the corner of Heath Hurst Road. The cabs have gone but the name Rumbold lives on.

South End Road, *c.* 1900. The Round House covered a steam pumping engine used to help supply London's water. In 1870 it was converted to a private house, and in 1907 it was demolished.

Above: Hampstead Picture Playhouse, South End Green, *c.* 1918. This cinema had 1,100 seats. It later became the Playhouse and then the Classic; it was remodelled to include three screens in 1978. *Left*: *c.* 1970. *Below*: 2002. The Royal Free Hospital towers over the cinema.

The White Horse public house, *c.* 1907. Constantine Road, left, and Fleet Road, right, were built in 1904 by Albert Pridmore. Today this is a very busy junction, which uses the zebra crossings as traffic management.

Fleet Road at the junction with Agincourt Road (right) and Southampton Road (left), *c.* 1910. Today the left side of the road is a play area.

Fleet Road, *c*. 1905. This photograph was taken looking towards Mansfield Road.

Cressy Road, near the junction with Agincourt Road, *c.* 1905. The Hampstead Model Laundry was one of the many laundries in the Hampstead area. A London ambulance station now occupies the site.

Agincourt Road, *c.* 1910. This picture, taken from Constantine Road, shows a horse-drawn tram heading into London. In 2002 a double-decker bus is on the same route.

4

Belsize Park

Charles Hendrick, Baker, 44 Englands Lane, Belsize Park, *c.* 1912. The driver is standing proudly by the vehicle. As a sub-manor of Hampstead, Belsize Manor was owned by one family from 1663 until 1807, when it was sold, divided and then developed into the area we know today.

Belsize Parade on Haverstock Hill, at the junction with Glenloch Road, *c.* 1910. The view in summer 2002 is much the same, with all the shops and flats surviving.

Haverstock Hill, at the corner with Belsize Avenue, *c.* 1930. The photograph shows the Vandervells garage and engineering works. The Holiday Inn, formerly the Post House Hotel, opened in 1970, together with a BP petrol station.

The Odeon, Haverstock Hill, *c.* 1938. The Odeon opened on 29 September 1934, housing a Compton organ and 1,544 seats. It was closed for thirteen years after suffering bomb damage in 1941, and finally closed in September 1972. *Opposite*: the Odeon, *c.* 1940. *Below*: Today the Odeon has been replaced by Budgens. There is, however, a cinema in the building next door called the Screen on the Hill. Of a much smaller capacity, it shows films of a less popular nature.

Haverstock Hill, showing the old Hampstead Town
Hall, built in 1877. Today the building is used as a
centre for community operations in the arts and
media.

Englands Lane from Eton Avenue, *c*. 1905. On the left is the Washington public house, which was built in about 1865, at the same time as the shops, by Daniel Tidey.

Englands Lane, looking towards Eton Avenue, *c.* 1905. The private road on the left is Chalcot Gardens, named after Upper Chalcots Farm, which was at the end of Englands Lane in 1745.

Belsize Park Terrace, Belsize Village, *c.* 1905. The roundabout has since been pedestrianised to help create a village feel, which is added to by the shops and restaurants.

Upper Belsize Terrace, *c.* 1905. The terrace was built by William Willet, who gave up some land in order to create the village green.

Belsize Crescent, *c.* 1900. This beautiful crescent leading off Belsize Park Terrace is tree-lined, and of course car-lined, today.

Belsize Park, *c.* 1920. In the background can be seen the tower of St Peter's, Belsize Park. Today the road layout has changed, and a paved area has been added. The church can just be seen above the trees.

The horse-drawn taxi cabs waiting for passengers outside Belsize Park station, *c.* 1910. Opened in 1907, it was part of the Charing Cross, Euston and Hampstead Railway. The stations all have oxblood red tiles. Under the station are two tunnels belonging to the Ministry of Defence, which still have steel bunk beds in place.

5

West Hampstead

Fortune Green, *c.* 1900. At the beginning of the nineteenth century this part of Hampstead
contained the tiny hamlets of West End Green and Fortune Green. It is bordered by
the Edgware Road (Watling Street) and by the Finchley Road (also an ancient track).
In common with other parts of London, the development of this area followed the arrival
of the railways.

Achilles Road, *c.* 1910. Ajax Road and Fortune Green are on the right.

Fortune Green, *c.* 1908. On the right is Salmon and Sons, sweetseller and newsvendor. Its name and title have changed but it remains in the same trade, having been replaced today by Angies Newsagent.

Fortune Green Road, *c.* 1905. This picture is taken from Achilles Road looking towards Burrard Road. The busy scene today includes the renowned Nautilus fish bar on the right.

Fortune Green Road, *c.* 1908. Architecturally these two pictures are very much alike, although a few modern buildings have been added. Further up on the left is the West Hampstead police station, which opened in 1972.

West End Lane and West End Green, at the junction with Fortune Green Road, looking towards the Finchley Road, *c.* 1905. In 2002 roadworks are adding to the problems at this busy junction.

West End Lane, *c.* 1914. An open-top bus is parked on the Green. In 2002 a single-decker bus is at the stop.

Mill Lane, *c.* 1900. These photographs, taken at the junction with Aldred Road, show that the parade has been carefully maintained. The concrete signs on the sides of the building show 'The Pavement 1888' and 'St Georges House, Aldred Road'.

West Hampstead fire station, West End Green, *c.* 1905. The fire station is dated 1901 and was designed by W.A. Scott. The pictures contrast two horse-drawn fire tenders ready for action almost a century ago with today's fire engine.

West End Green, *c.* 1903. The photograph shows a typical Edwardian scene with cycles, pedestrians and hand-drawn carts using the road in safety. The traffic rate has increased considerably. In the modern photograph the fire station is on the right.

West End Lane, *c.* 1910. This is the bridge over what is now the Thameslink line. The scene today is a mixture of old and new together.

West End Lane, with West Hampstead station on the left. The Metropolitan Railway opened this station on 30 June 1879. The Bakerloo line started on 20 November 1939. In 1979 it became part of the new Jubilee line.

West End Lane, *c.* 1900. The photograph shows the police station, which was on this site from 1882 to 1972, when the police moved to Fortune Green Road. *Below*: the same view today.

West End Lane, *c.* 1920. These photographs are taken looking north, with Broadhurst Gardens on the right. The bank in the picture above is a food and wine store today.

6

South Hampstead

Swiss Cottage Tavern, *c.* 1902. This was one of the earliest buildings in the area. It stood near the site of the old tollgate on the Finchley Road, which was removed in 1871. The photograph shows one of the 'express' buses, which ran from Swiss Cottage to the Bank. A flat fare of *6d* was charged for any distance.

Fitzjohns Avenue, near the junction with College Crescent, 1906. Between 1851 and 1900 Hampstead's population rose from 12,000 to 80,000 and many new roads were constructed. In 1875 Fitzjohns Avenue was planned to form a link from Finchley Road to the village of Hampstead. The new road ran across what was then farmland.

West Hampstead Congregational church, Finchley Road, showing the corner of Burrard Road, *c.* 1912. The church has been converted into flats called The Octagon.

Hampstead Public Library, Finchley Road, 1905. This building on the corner of Arkwright Road dates from 1897, and was replaced by the new library at Swiss Cottage in 1964. The old library was officially opened as an arts centre in 1966.

Finchley Road and Frognal station, *c.* 1904. This station opened on 2 January 1860 as Finchley Road (St John's Wood) and was renamed on 1 October 1880.

Taylor and Lown Ltd – Motor and Carriage Jobmasters' garage and head office, Rosemont Road, *c.* 1910. *Right*: an advertisement from *Kelly's Directory*, 1912. *Below*: Rosemont Road from the junction with the Finchley Road, 2002. The road is being resurfaced after extensive refurbishment to all of the buildings had taken place.

Finchley Road station, Finchley Road, 1903. The Metropolitan line opened in June 1879 and was joined by the Bakerloo line in 1939, when the station was rebuilt. This became part of the new Jubilee line on 1 May 1979. The picture below shows the new building as it is today.

Finchley Road, *c.* 1925. The photograph shows Trinity church on the right and the Finchley Road underground station in the centre. Today's photograph was taken from under the awning of Habitat.

John Barnes's store, Finchley Road, *c.* 1912. The building was replaced in the 1930s, and Habitat and Waitrose now occupy the site.

Above: The Odeon, Swiss Cottage, *c.* 1939. The Odeon opened on Saturday 4 September 1937 with 2,115 seats, which was large for an Odeon. It was modernised in about 1960 and converted into three cinemas in 1973. Later three further screens were added in the former front stalls, stage area and upstairs foyer, and the remodelled cinema was opened on 19 June 1992.

The Cross Roads, Swiss Cottage, looking towards College Crescent, *c.* 1920. Only the building in the centre has survived.

College Crescent, *c.* 1908. A policeman directs traffic at a nice spacious junction. Today there are traffic lights, barriers and more traffic.

Swiss Cottage station. This is situated at the junction of Swiss Terrace and the Finchley Road. The old station on the Metropolitan line was built in 1868 and officially closed on 18 August 1940. A new station, below the surface on the Bakerloo line, opened on 20 November 1939. This was transferred to the Jubilee line in 1979. In 2002 the only feature to remain is the spire of a distant church in the centre.

The Swiss Cottage, 1907. For a short period the horse-drawn buses of Hampstead shared the road with the new motor-buses. The last horse-drawn bus ran from London Bridge station to Moorgate station on 25 October 1911. In the 2002 photograph the entrance to the underground station can be seen on the left.

Adelaide Road, looking towards Chalk Farm, *c.* 1906. The cyclists only had to concern themselves with a horse and cart approaching; today things move considerably faster.

Primrose Hill Road, showing the bridge
over the railway lines, *c.* 1909. Beyond the
horse-drawn taxi on the right lies the
church of St Mary the Virgin, built in
1871–5 from the designs of M.P. Manning.

7
Chalk Farm

The area of Chalk Farm was mostly open fields with a couple of coaching inns until the late eighteenth century, when development started around the old coaching route to Hampstead.

Chalk Farm Road, *c.* 1912. The Enterprise public house is on the corner of Chalk Farm Road and Ferdinand Street, which is a direct route to South End Green. The building has not changed apart from a few of its fascia features, although the buildings around it have. The building to the left of The Enterprise is now used by the Salvation Army.

Chalk Farm Road, *c.* 1905. In the background of the photograph above Chalk Farm station is being built. The horse-drawn cab has been replaced in the photograph below with modern black cabs, as well as much larger buses. Some of the buildings have been demolished and a garage, to service modern transport, now stands in their place.

Chalk Farm Road, *c.* 1905. On the left are the yards and industrial buildings that came about when the Midland Railway line, which was mainly used for goods traffic, was extended from Chalk Farm to Euston. These buildings are now used for retail and antique shops.

The bridge over the Grand Junction Canal, and the railway bridge in the background, *c.* 1910. Although the horse-bus is full and there are people walking around, the picture below is quite a contrast. This is a typical weekend scene today: shoppers and tourists flock into the area for the market, open-fronted shops and atmosphere of this very busy area.

ACKNOWLEDGEMENTS & PICTURE CREDITS

Hampstead Past & Present has been a pleasure to complete. While the majority of the pictures are from the Memories Picture Library we have had some assistance, and special thanks go to Nicky Hillman, Tony Moss, Neal Garner and Rod Brewster.

The Memories collection started in the 1960s, when Clive Smith started collecting postcards of Hendon. In 1973 Clive published his first book, *Hendon As It Was*. This in turn created a demand in the area for pictures from the book and also more interest in local history. In 1979 the Hendon Collectors Centre was opened in Greyhound Hill where Clive sold postcards, books and reproductions from the collection. In 1981 the collection moved to a Bell Lane shop, where Clive and David continued publishing local books, including *Hampstead As It Was*, and selling pictures of the local area.

Memories Picture Library is now at 130/132 Brent Street, a large double-fronted shop on the main road in Hendon. Pictures, framing and old picture postcards are available. Clive's eldest son, David, who produces the photographic reproductions for the collection, has taken all the modern pictures for this book. Clive and David both started their careers in Fleet Street, Clive working in the library and David in the darkroom. They now work together at Memories collecting more pictures and preserving our local history.

Copies of the pictures from this book and all our publications are available from:
Memories Picture Library, 130/132 Brent Street, Hendon, London NW4 2DR
Tel 020 8203 1500 Fax 020 8203 7031
www.memoriespostcards.co.uk

By the same authors

Holly Place and St Mary's Church, *c.* 1911.